THE **33.3**

PRAYER CHALLENGE

—— A PERSONAL INVITATION FROM GOD ——

THE 33:3 PRAYER CHALLENGE

A PERSONAL INVITATION FROM GOD

33 DEVOTIONS TO SPARK
POWERFUL AND PERSISTENT PRAYER

SHERWOOD H. PATTERSON

 QUEST PRESS

To the faithful and fervent prayer warriors of Quest Church. May your prayers ignite a movement of spiritual revival among God's people.

Introduction

Twelve years later, I can still remember it like yesterday—teaching my daughter to ride her bike for the first time. Her little hands gripped the handlebars so tightly, and her eyes were wide with nervous determination. She kept glancing back at me as I reassured her, "I've got you." Running alongside her, I held the seat to keep her steady as the wobbles began. She pedaled hesitantly, her balance unsteady, her movements uncertain. And then, before either of us could react, she veered off course and crashed into a parked car. I gasped, rushing to her side, but thankfully, she was okay—just a bit startled. She brushed herself off, got back on the bike, and tried again. Over time, with more attempts and plenty of encouragement, she mastered the art of riding. What once seemed impossible became second nature.

Prayer is much like that first bike ride. Initially, it can feel awkward and unfamiliar, like trying to keep balance on two wheels for the first time. We might stumble in our words, feel uncertain of what to say, or even crash into moments of doubt or discouragement. Yet, just like learning to ride, prayer requires practice and persistence. Over time, it transforms from something we struggle to do into something as natural as breathing. Eventually, we find ourselves "coasting along," so to speak, enjoying the ride of intimate conversation with God. We learn to release control, trust Him, and even marvel at the excitement of the journey.

The beauty of prayer is that we are never learning alone. Just as I ran alongside my daughter, steadying her when she wobbled and comforting her when she crashed, our Heavenly Father is with us every step of the way. His presence brings us confidence when we feel nervous, strength to get back up when we falter, and guidance to steer us in the right direction. As we grow in prayer, we are reminded that He delights in the process, cheering us on as we go. And as we practice and persevere, prayer becomes not just something we do, but a joyful rhythm of life where we feel God's steadying hand, even when we take our hands off the handlebars.

You see, prayer is not just a spiritual conversation but a personal invitation from God. One of my life verses is Jeremiah 33:3: *"Call to me and I will answer you, and show you great and mighty things, which you do not know."* This verse has always left me in awe and wonder. For starters, it absolutely blows me away that the God of the universe—the Creator of galaxies, oceans, and every living thing—would desire to engage in a personal and intimate relationship with me. It's humbling to think that the One who holds all things together extends an invitation to commune with Him in prayer. That simple, yet profound, truth stirs my heart every time I reflect on it.

The vastness of God's power and knowledge is completely unfathomable to me. His wisdom is beyond comprehension, and His works are too magnificent to fully grasp. Yet, in His greatness, He seeks us out and actively invites us to approach Him. What's even more mind-blowing is that He hears and responds to our cries. This reveals so much about who God is—not distant, indifferent, or unreachable, but loving, caring, and compassionate. Knowing that He listens and cares for every detail of my life reassures me that He is on my side and for me. That truth encourages me to call out to Him with confidence, trusting that my prayers matter to Him.

What amazes me most is that this mighty God, who reveals Himself to us, responds with great and mighty things that we could never imagine. As we seek Him in prayer, He works out the events of our lives in ways that bring about His glory and our good. I've seen Him answer prayers in ways far beyond what I could ask or think, and I've seen Him reveal Himself through challenges and victories alike. This verse reminds me that prayer is a divine get-a-way to experiencing God's power and presence. As we trust Him and walk with Him in prayer, we discover the beauty of His plans unfolding in our lives, reminding us that He truly is a God who does far more than we can imagine.

Look, I get it, as a pastor I'm supposed to encourage people to pray. But let me tell you, I learned early on in ministry that God desires to do a good work in me before He ever does a great work through me. So, I strive to humbly live, practice, and model the way of Jesus in my personal life and ministry calling. That doesn't mean I'm perfect, but I'm still being perfected. Prayer isn't just something I preach about, it's the heartbeat of my relationship with God, and something I continue to learn about and grow in. This conviction has deepened as I've studied revival movements throughout church history and discovered that every powerful move of God begins with ordinary people humbling themselves before an extraordinary God.

As a student of revival movements, I've always been intrigued by the ways God has worked through history to awaken His church. What stands out in all these movements is a fresh awareness of personal sin and repentance, a reinvigorating hunger for God's Word, and an ignition of powerful, persistent prayer. These common threads have inspired my own ministry and fueled my longing to see God move in mighty ways today. At Quest Church, where I have the privilege to pastor, we took the invitation of Jeremiah 33:3

seriously, believing that when we call to God, He answers and reveals things beyond our imagination. In response, we dedicated 33 days to extended prayer and fasting, earnestly seeking God's presence. And let me tell you, the power of God fell on His people as we devoted ourselves to faithful and fervent prayer. It was a season of awakening, marked by a deeper dependence on Him and a renewed passion for His purposes.

During those 33 days, I felt a personal stirring to go even deeper into my own study of prayer. I began writing daily devotions and reflecting on key principles of prayer that shaped not only my personal walk with God, but also the collective spiritual revival we experienced as a church. These writings eventually turned into this book, birthed from a desire to spark the same fervency and passion for prayer in others. My prayer is that these Biblical devotions will ignite a hunger for revival in hearts across our nation and around the world. Prayer is the spark that lights the flame of revival, and my hope is that this book will inspire you to seek God like never before, trusting Him to reveal His great and mighty plans for your life and His church.

This devotional can be used for personal growth, or as a tool to help your church spark powerful and persistent prayer. When we initiated our 33 days of prayer and fasting at Quest Church, we created intentional opportunities to seek God together. Every day at 3:33 pm, we opened the church for anyone available to gather and pray in person. At the same time, we encouraged everyone—whether they could come in person or not—to set a daily reminder on their phones for 3:33 pm. When the alarm went off, we asked them to pause and pray wherever they were for three things: first, to praise God for who He is or what He has done in their lives; second, to pray for someone they know who needed God's comfort or care; and third, to pray for a specific personal need. It was amazing to hear how these 3:33 prayer breaks not only helped people establish a daily rhythm of prayer, but also opened the door to divine appointments to encourage and minister to others in unexpected ways.

We also encouraged everyone to prayerfully consider making a personal commitment to fasting during this time. Each person chose how they would fast—some gave up social media, others fasted technology, and still others fasted meals or certain types of food. The impact of fasting was undeniable. As people gave up things they relied on or valued, they experienced an increased urgency and dependency on God. Many shared how the fast brought them into a deeper awareness of His presence and peace, while also unleashing His power in their lives. What began as personal sacrifices, became a powerful collective experience of leaning into God's strength. Through prayer and fasting, we saw lives transformed, families restored, and hearts awakened to God's purposes.

Imagine what God could do in your life in just 33 days if you committed yourself fully to prayer. Whether you use this devotional on your own or with your church, these daily reflections, prayer principles, and guided prayers are designed to spark a movement of spiritual revival. Everything in your life can be fundamentally changed as you devote yourself to seeking God wholeheartedly. As you follow these steps, may you encounter the transforming presence of God, discover His plans for your life, and experience His peace and power in new and profound ways. My prayer is that these 33 days will ignite a deeper passion for prayer, and an enduring hunger for God that doesn't stop when the 33 days are over, but continues to grow, bringing revival in your heart, home, church, and community.

PRAYER
PRINCIPLE

—————— 01 ——————

*God receives and responds
to the prayers of His people
with profound revelation.*

--- **DAY 1** ---

God Hears Our Prayers

"Call to Me, and I will answer you, and show you great and mighty things, which you do not know."

JEREMIAH 33:3

Before modern technology, making a phone call was quite the process. In the early days of telephone systems, operators were responsible for manually connecting one line to another using switchboards and cables. A person wishing to make a call would be patched into the network by a dispatcher, allowing a voice connection between two people. Although this method required some work, it ultimately provided a reliable way to communicate across distances.

This process of telephone communication can serve as a metaphor for prayer. Prayer is our way of being "patched in" directly to God. Unlike the old telephone systems, where calls could be dropped or signals might fail, prayer offers us a direct, clear, and uninterrupted connection to the throne room of heaven. We don't need a middleman or a complex system to get through to God—He is always ready to hear our prayers.

In Jeremiah 33:3, we find the prophet Jeremiah imprisoned for his faithful ministry, and Israel devastated by the Babylonian conquest. The people are in exile, the city is in ruins, and hope seems lost. Yet in the midst of this overwhelming situation, God speaks. He invites Jeremiah—and by extension, all of His people—to call upon Him. God's promise is twofold: first, that He will answer, and second, that He will reveal "great and mighty things" that they do not yet know.

This was a message of profound hope and assurance. Although Jeremiah's physical circumstances were bleak, God's promise was one of restoration and healing. He assured Jeremiah that beyond the devastation and destruction, He had plans for healing, health, and a future. In the same way, when we cry out to God in prayer, He hears us, even in the midst of our deepest struggles.

Sometimes we feel as though our prayers are ineffective, or perhaps we wonder if God is even listening. Jeremiah 33:3 reminds us that not only does God hear us, but He also promises to respond. His response may not always look the way we expect, but it is always filled with His truth, wisdom, and love. He reveals to us things that are beyond our limited understanding, and gives us insight into His greater purposes.

When we pray, God graciously pulls back the curtain, allowing us to see glimpses of His divine plan. While we may not always comprehend everything, we can trust that His will is good and that He works for the benefit of His people. Just as God offered hope to Jeremiah and Israel, He offers us hope through prayer. He invites us to call upon Him, and when we do, He answers with peace, revelation, and purpose.

So, let's take hold of this invitation. When we cry out to God, we are connecting directly with the Creator who holds all things in His hands. And in His perfect time, He reveals the "great and mighty things" He has planned for us.

PRAYER PAUSE

*Heavenly Father, thank You for hearing
me when I pray. Help me trust in
Your timing and see beyond my own
understanding. Reveal Your plans for
my life, and give me faith to hold onto
Your promises, knowing You are always
working for my good. Amen*

PRAYER POINTS

- Praise God that he hears our prayers and responds with His profound truths.

_____

_____

- Pray for three people by name who are desperate to hear from God in their lives.

_____

_____

- Pray that God would stir in you a fervent passion to seek God in prayer.

_____

_____

PRAYER
PRINCIPLE

—— 02 ——

Prayer tethers us to the
influence and guidance
of the Holy Spirit.

—— DAY 2 ——
Help from the Holy Spirit

"Likewise the Spirit also helps in our weaknesses. For we do not know what we should pray for as we ought, but the Spirit Himself makes intercession for us with groanings which cannot be uttered."

ROMANS 8:26

David Brown, the world's fastest blind sprinter, holds multiple world records and has competed in three Paralympic Games. His incredible speed is made possible through a deep partnership with his guide runner, Jeremy Avery. The two are connected by a short tether and run in perfect sync. Jeremy gives David verbal cues to help him stay on course, guiding him through every step of the race. With every stride, their feet hit the ground at the same time, making them appear as one runner in motion. David doesn't need to worry about straying too far or falling behind—his only focus is on listening to his guide's voice and following his lead.

This powerful image of trust and partnership is a beautiful reminder of how we can experience prayer with the help of the Holy Spirit. Romans 8:26 tells us that the Holy Spirit "helps in our weaknesses" and "makes intercession for us." Just like David relies on Jeremy's verbal cues and the tether to run the race, we are tethered to the Holy Spirit, who guides and directs our prayers according to God's will.

Sometimes life's pressures, challenges, and overwhelming circumstances make it difficult to know how to pray or what to ask for. Worry and fear can creep in, causing us to either pray from a place of our own wisdom and strength or, worse, to abandon prayer altogether. Yet this verse offers tremendous encouragement: we don't have to rely on our own understanding or ability. In prayer, the Holy Spirit comes alongside us, just like a guide runner, helping to carry the weight of our uncertainty and aligning our prayers with God's heart.

Remarkably, the Holy Spirit takes an active role in our prayer life, ensuring that our prayers don't veer off course or fall short of what God desires. Even when we feel weak or unsure, the Spirit intercedes for us in prayer with words that go beyond our own human abilities, carrying our deepest needs and desires to the throne of grace.

Prayer is not just a monologue of our thoughts and feelings. It's a partnership, a synchronization between our prayers and the Holy Spirit's providence. Every day, as we bring our hearts before God, we can walk in step with the Spirit, trusting Him to guide our prayers toward God's perfect will. Just as David Brown's feet stay in sync with Jeremy Avery's during a race, our prayers remain in sync with God's purposes when we are tethered to the Holy Spirit.

This passage encourages us to approach prayer with confidence, knowing that we don't walk—or pray—alone. We are never left to figure things out by ourselves. With the Holy Spirit's help, we can pray with assurance, knowing that He is always there, guiding us, aligning us with God's will, and leading us forward, step by step.

PRAYER PAUSE

Dear God, thank You for the gift and guidance of the Holy Spirit. Help me to stay connected to His leading in my life and depend upon the Holy Spirit to align my prayers with Your will. Give me confidence to walk in step with the Holy Spirit every day. Amen

PRAYER POINTS

- Praise God for the assistance, assurance, and counsel of the Holy Spirit.

_____

_____

- Pray for three people by name who are in need of the comfort of the Holy Spirit.

_____

_____

- Pray for three specific areas of your life where the Holy Spirit can give you guidance.

_____

_____

PRAYER
PRINCIPLE

—— 03 ——

We need regular prayer pit stops to refuel spiritually and refocus clearly on God.

Prayer Pit Stops

"So He Himself often withdrew into the wilderness and prayed."

LUKE 5:16

Long-distance race car driving is an endurance sport that pushes both the driver and the car to their limits. These finely tuned machines are designed to withstand grueling track conditions, but the longer they stay on the track, the more their effectiveness diminishes. The intense speeds, sharp turns, and constant friction wear down the tires, burn up fuel, and leave the windshield streaked with dirt. To remain competitive, race cars need periodic pit stops to refuel, replace worn tires, clean the windshield for a clear view, and repair any damage sustained during the race.

Without these essential pit stops, even the most finely engineered race car would not make it to the finish line. The pit stops enable the car to regain peak performance, ready to tackle the next stretch of the race.

In Luke 5:16, we learn that Jesus Himself, despite His divinity and tireless ministry, made regular "pit stops" in prayer. As He raced through the demands of His public ministry—teaching, healing, and caring for multitudes—He often withdrew to quiet, solitary places to refuel in the presence of His Father. Jesus understood that His power, wisdom, and strength came not from His own human effort, but from His connection with God through prayer.

Just like race cars need periodic maintenance, we too need regular "prayer pit stops" to refuel our spirits and clear our minds. The high speeds and pressures of life can wear us down. As we navigate the twists and turns of relationships, work, challenges, and personal struggles, our spiritual tanks can run empty, our vision can become clouded, and our strength can be depleted.

Jesus' example shows us the importance of pausing to spend time in prayer. Through prayer, we are spiritually refueled for the next round of challenges, equipped with God's strength to persevere, and able to remove the distractions that block our ability to see Him clearly. Without these times of refreshment, we risk burnout, frustration, and losing sight of God's purposes in our lives.

In prayer, God repairs the broken places in our hearts, fills us with His peace, and restores our focus on His truth. Prayer gives us the spiritual stamina we need to endure and run the race of life with faith and endurance. No matter how busy or pressured we may feel, we are never too busy to follow Jesus' example and pull into the pit stop of prayer.

Taking time to pause and pray doesn't slow us down—it empowers us to run the race with greater effectiveness and endurance. Prayer is the pit stop that prepares us for the path ahead.

PRAYER PAUSE

Heavenly Father, help me to follow Jesus' example of seeking You in the midst of life's demands. Teach me to slow down and make time for prayer so that I can be refueled by Your strength and see Your guidance clearly in every challenge I face. Amen.

PRAYER POINTS

- Praise God for His willingness to repair, refuel, and restore our lives through prayer.

_____

_____

- Pray for three people by name who need God's strength to empower them in their lives.

_____

_____

- Pray for a heart to slow down and seek to spend more time in God's restoring presence.

_____

_____

PRAYER PRINCIPLE

04

*Prayer exchanges our
momentary pressures for
God's constant peace.*

—— **DAY 4** ——

Peace in Life's Pressures

*"Be anxious for nothing, but in everything by prayer
and supplication, with thanksgiving, let your
requests be made known to God; and the peace of
God, which surpasses all understanding, will guard
your hearts and minds through Christ Jesus."*

PHILIPPIANS 4:6-7

Anxiety, depression, and loneliness are at an all-time high in today's world. According to recent statistics, over 40 million adults in the U.S. experience some form of anxiety each year, with depression affecting nearly 8% of the population. Loneliness, often amplified by social isolation and stress, has become a common struggle. In response to these overwhelming pressures, many people turn to temporary solutions like substances, unhealthy relationships, or even isolation, hoping to numb their pain. However, these methods only deepen the problem, leaving them even more desperate and broken.

Every person faces some level of anxiety or fear in life—whether it's financial stress, health concerns, relational conflicts, or uncertainties about the future. The human heart is always searching for ways to deal with these intense emotions. Philippians 4:6-7 offers us a clear solution: prayer. God's Word doesn't just acknowledge our anxieties; it shows us the path to peace.

This passage calls us to bring everything to God in prayer, no matter how small or overwhelming. Instead of carrying the heavy burdens of worry, fear, or stress on our own, we are invited to lay them at God's feet. Prayer becomes the exchange point where the pressures of life are lifted and replaced by God's unshakable peace.

In prayer, we are invited to be honest and transparent before God, bringing Him all our worries, concerns, and needs. But it's not just a dumping ground for our anxieties. It's also an opportunity to thank God for His goodness, faithfulness, and provision—even in the middle of our difficulties. This act of thanksgiving shifts our focus from our problems to the power and presence of God.

God promises that when we pray and cast our cares on Him, His peace—"which surpasses all understanding"—will guard our hearts and minds. This peace isn't temporary or based on circumstances; it's a deep, abiding sense of calm that comes from trusting God. His peace serves as a protective shield over our thoughts and emotions, keeping us grounded in faith rather than overwhelmed by fear.

When we make prayer a regular practice in our lives, we are reminded that we don't have to walk through life's pressures alone. God hears us, cares for us, and provides a peace that the world cannot give. As we learn to trust Him fully, we can experience the comfort and strength that come from knowing He is in control.

PRAYER PAUSE

Heavenly Father, I come to You with all my worries, fears, and anxieties. I lay them at Your feet, trusting that You care for me. Thank You for Your peace that guards my heart and mind, and help me to continue trusting You in every situation. Amen.

PRAYER POINTS

◆ Praise God for His abundant peace in the midst of life's overwhelming pressures.

_____

_____

◆ Pray for three people by name who need God's peace to guard their hearts and minds.

_____

_____

◆ In prayer, give God your worries and anxieties and trust His goodness and faithfulness.

_____

_____

PRAYER
PRINCIPLE

—————— **05** ——————

*Revival begins when we
humble ourselves in prayer
and seek God's face.*

————————————————

—— **DAY 5** ——

Spiritual Revival

*"If My people who are called by My name
will humble themselves, and pray and seek
My face, and turn from their wicked ways,
then I will hear from heaven, and will forgive
their sin and heal their land."*

2 CHRONICLES 7:14

The defibrillator is a life-saving device used to deliver an electrical shock to the heart in emergencies like cardiac arrest. This shock is designed to restart the heart's rhythm and bring it back to its normal function. In critical situations, when the heart stops or beats irregularly, this jolt of electricity can make the difference between life and death. Just as a defibrillator revives a heart in distress, prayer is God's tool for reviving our souls when we've drifted dangerously far from Him.

2 Chronicles 7:14 is an appeal for spiritual revival—a wake-up call for those who have fallen into spiritual complacency or rebellion. In this passage, God speaks directly to His people, reminding them that if they humble themselves, turn from their sins, and seek Him in prayer, He will respond with forgiveness and healing. The context of this verse is rooted in God's covenant relationship with Israel. After Solomon dedicated the temple, God made this promise to His people:

if they strayed from Him and faced judgment, there was still a path to restoration through repentance and prayer.

This principle applies to God's people today. Whether as individuals or as a society, we often find ourselves in need of spiritual revival. Sometimes, it feels like our hearts have grown cold, and we've wandered from God's ways. It's easy to become spiritually "numb," just like a heart that needs a defibrillator to restart. In these moments, God offers us a way back through prayer.

God uses humble, repentant prayer to shock our hearts back into spiritual alignment. No matter how far we have drifted, He stands ready to restore us. We might be facing grim personal circumstances or even national or global crisis, but God promises that when we turn to Him in sincere repentance, He will bring life and healing. This verse shows us that revival doesn't come from programs, plans, or strategies—it begins with the passionate prayers of God's people.

That's why significant revival delays, where fervent prayer decays. If we desire to see transformation in our lives, families, communities, and even nations, it must begin with humble, heartfelt prayer. God doesn't just want surface-level change; He wants to heal our deepest wounds, cleanse us from sin, and revive us with His life-giving Spirit. But that revival begins when we, His people, seek Him in prayer.

This verse is a powerful reminder that God desires to forgive, heal, and restore us, but we must be willing to call on Him. He promises to respond to our cries, and when He does, it brings a life-giving jolt to our souls that leads to spiritual renewal.

PRAYER PAUSE

*Lord, I come before You humbly,
seeking Your forgiveness and healing.
Revive my heart, renew my spirit, and
bring Your restoration to my life, my
family, and my community. Help me to
seek You daily in prayer. Amen.*

PRAYER POINTS

- Praise God that He is gracious to restore His people when they call out to Him.

_____

_____

- Pray for three people by name who need God's healing touch on their lives.

_____

_____

- Confess your sins to God in prayer and receive His forgiveness and healing.

_____

_____

PRAYER
PRINCIPLE

—— 06 ——

Prayer is a powerful weapon
that equips us for spiritual
warfare and defends against
wicked attacks.

Weapons of War

"Praying always with all prayer and supplication in the Spirit, being watchful to this end with all perseverance and supplication for all the saints."

EPHESIANS 6:18

In warfare, military generals plan their campaigns with precision and care, considering every possible strategy to defend their positions and gain ground against the enemy. They study their opponent's tactics, anticipate their moves, and search for weaknesses to exploit. The success of a military campaign often depends on how effectively a general employs both defensive measures to protect against attacks and offensive strategies to strike the enemy.

As Christians, we are engaged in a similar battle—not against flesh and blood, but in the spiritual realm. Ephesians 6:12 reminds us that we fight against principalities, powers, and the rulers of darkness. This war is not one we can see, but it is very real. The enemy of our souls, Satan, seeks to deceive, manipulate, and destroy us. He studies our weaknesses and looks for ways to attack. But just as military generals prepare for battle with the right tools and strategies, God has equipped us with powerful spiritual weapons to stand firm.

Ephesians 6 describes the armor of God: the belt of truth, the breastplate of righteousness, the shield of faith, and more. But one of the most powerful offensive weapons we have is prayer. Prayer is not just a tool for personal comfort—it is a weapon of war, designed to defend against the schemes of the enemy and to advance God's kingdom. Just as generals communicate with their troops and headquarters for guidance, we communicate with God through prayer to receive His direction and power.

Prayer empowers us to stand firm in the face of the enemy's attacks, no matter how fierce. When we face the lies of the enemy, prayer helps us discern the truth. When we feel weak, prayer gives us the strength to keep going. Prayer also allows us to fight for others. We are instructed to pray for "all the saints"—to lift up our brothers and sisters who are also under attack and in need of God's protection.

In the heat of spiritual battle, no situation is too big or too small to take to God in prayer. Whether it's daily challenges or moments of intense spiritual warfare, we are called to pray with perseverance. Like great battlefield generals, we must recognize that success in this spiritual campaign comes from depending on God's power, not our own. Prayer keeps us connected to God's strength, and it gives us the upper hand in spiritual warfare.

As we engage in this spiritual battle, we can be confident that through prayer, God is not only protecting us, but also equipping us to stand firm and fight for His kingdom and cause.

PRAYER PAUSE

Lord, thank You for equipping me with the tools I need for this spiritual battle. Help me to rely on Your strength in prayer and to stand firm against the enemy. Empower me to fight for others through prayer and to always seek You for guidance. Amen.

PRAYER POINTS

- Praise God that He has given us prayer as a powerful weapon against our enemy.

_____

_____

- Pray for three people by name who are experiencing spiritual battles.

_____

_____

- Ask God for His protection and that He would help you stay alert to fight every battle in prayer.

_____

_____

PRAYER
PRINCIPLE

—— 07 ——

Lifting our eyes to God in prayer reminds us that His power is greater than any problem we face.

— DAY 7 —

Above it all

"In this manner, therefore, pray: Our Father in heaven, hallowed be Your name."

MATTHEW 6:9

Few things in nature captivate our attention like the stunning beauty of a rainbow. After an intense storm, where clouds darken the sky, winds blow fiercely, and rain falls heavily, a rainbow often appears as a vibrant arc painted across the heavens. Its brilliant colors remind us that the storm has passed and brighter days are on the horizon. Rainbows have a way of drawing our gaze upward, pausing our busyness as we stand in awe of this symbol of peace, hope, and promise.

In Matthew 6:9, Jesus teaches us to start our prayers with a focus on God's position and character. Like the rainbow, which stretches high above us after a storm, God's sovereign place "in heaven" reminds us that He is far above the challenges and storms we face on earth. No matter how fierce or unyielding our struggles feel, God's authority and love are far-reaching, extending over every situation. When we acknowledge that God is our Father in heaven, we shift our focus from the turmoil around us to the One who reigns above it all.

This beginning to the Lord's Prayer encourages us to lift our eyes above life's "storm clouds" to see our loving, active, and sovereign Father. He is intimately involved in our lives, yet He sits above every earthly circumstance, fully capable of bringing peace, comfort, and restoration. When we begin our prayers by recognizing God's holy position, we're reminded that what feels overwhelming to us is well within His control. Prayer, in this way, invites us to trust that whatever is over our heads, remains under God's feet.

However, before we present our requests or petitions, Jesus directs us to start with adoration—acknowledging God's greatness, goodness, and worthiness of our praise. This approach not only honors God, but also prepares our hearts to align with His will and purposes. In prayer, as we focus on our Heavenly Father, our perspective shifts. Rather than being absorbed by our worries, we find peace in God's faithful nature, knowing that He's the same powerful Creator who spoke the rainbow into existence. As a result, our hearts are strengthened when we remember that we're loved and cared for by the One who holds the universe.

These promises in prayer reveals God's prominence over our petitions, causing us to pause and gaze at His radiant beauty and His steadfast provision. Just as we can't help but stop and admire the rainbow, our prayers should begin with a moment of awe at who God is. When we come to Him in prayer, lifting our eyes to our Father in heaven, we find that He is already aware of our needs, already holding us through the storm, and already preparing the bright hope that lies beyond.

PRAYER PAUSE

Heavenly Father, I come to You in awe of Your greatness and glory. Help me to lift my eyes above my troubles, trusting that You are above it all and that nothing escapes Your care. Let Your majesty fill my heart with peace and confidence today. Amen.

PRAYER POINTS

◆ Praise God for His all-powerful and sovereign nature to control every detail of your life.

_____

_____

◆ Pray for three people by name who need to surrender and submit to God's authority.

_____

_____

◆ Place all your cares and concerns into the loving and capable hands of your Heavenly Father.

_____

_____

PRAYER PRINCIPLE

08

The best way to taste God's goodness is to mix together hope, patience, and prayer into our lives.

—— **DAY 8** ——

The Right Ingredients

*"Rejoicing in hope, patient in tribulation, continuing
steadfastly in prayer."*

ROMANS 12:12

There's something comforting and heartwarming about
your mom's favorite meal. It's not just the taste; it's
the way it feels—comforting, satisfying, and rich with
familiar flavors. You may have even tried to replicate it by
following her recipe, measuring each ingredient exactly,
but somehow, it's just not quite the same. That's because
your mom doesn't really need the recipe—she knows it
by heart, adding a pinch here, a dash there, and a splash
of love that somehow pulls everything together perfectly.

In Romans 12:12, God gives us His own "recipe" for a fulfilling
and abundant life. This verse lays out the "ingredients" that
blend together for a life that stands firm through every trial: a
generous measure of joy, a pinch of patience, and a persistent
prayer life. Like any good recipe, it's the balance and
combination of these ingredients that make all the difference.

First, God calls us to rejoice in hope. Hope is like the
sweetness that enhances every part of the recipe. Even in
tough times, joy reminds us of God's goodness and promises.

Just like the warmth and familiarity of a favorite meal, hope anchors us in the strength and assurance that God is at work, even when we can't see it. Joy in hope is the foundational flavor that keeps us steady and strengthens our faith.

Next, a heaping pinch of patience allows our hearts to rest and grow in times of adversity. Just as dough must rise to reach its full potential, patience allows us to endure, confident that God is perfecting us and working everything out for our good. In challenging times, patience helps us avoid "rushing the recipe" and gives our hearts time to develop peace and resilience, even as the heat of trials intensifies.

Finally, prayer ties everything together. Just as all the right ingredients must be combined to create a beautiful dish, prayer keeps our hearts connected to God's purposes and allows His power to work in our lives. Steady, ongoing prayer isn't a once-and-done activity—it's a daily practice that, over time, transforms bitterness into a sweet and satisfying life. Through prayer, we're able to taste and see the goodness of God, even in life's hardest moments.

Life can be filled with bitterness from hopeless situations or sour seasons of suffering. Yet, by faithfully following God's recipe of joy, patience, and persistent prayer, we can overcome and allow His grace to turn each season into something meaningful and beautiful. When we live according to His recipe, we become a sweet and savory expression of His flavor and favor, bringing a taste of God's goodness to a world in need. Let's embrace God's ingredients and allow Him to perfect the recipe for our lives, creating something truly satisfying and whole.

PRAYER PAUSE

*Heavenly Father, thank You for giving
me the recipe for a fulfilling, abundant
life. Help me to rejoice in hope, remain
patient in trials, and turn to You
continually in prayer. Fill my heart
with joy and patience as I trust in Your
perfect plans. Amen.*

PRAYER POINTS

♦ Praise God that He fills us with joy and patience to endure every trial and hardship.

_____

_____

♦ Pray for three people by name who are struggling to experience God's joy.

_____

_____

♦ Pray for more joy and patience as you seek God steadfastly in prayer.

_____

_____

PRAYER PRINCIPLE

—————— 09 ——————

*Praying for others brings uplifting
strength when the pressures of life
are bearing down.*

———————————————

DAY 9

Burden Bearers

"Confess your trespasses to one another, and pray for one another, that you may be healed. The effective, fervent prayer of a righteous man avails much."

JAMES 5:16

Watching a powerful weightlifter press hundreds of pounds over their chest is a striking image of strength, focus, and determination. Yet, as strong as these athletes are, they always have a spotter nearby. This spotter stands close to the lifter, providing encouragement and support as they strive to lift more than ever before. The spotter knows that with each added pound, the risk and difficulty increase. They remain ready to offer encouragement, help guide the weight, and most importantly, catch the barbell if the lifter can no longer hold it alone. Without the help of a spotter, the lifter could be crushed under the weight if fatigue sets in or they lose their grip.

James 5:16 calls us to be "spotters" for one another in life. We're encouraged to pray for one another, bearing each other's burdens and providing spiritual support during life's heavy moments. Like weightlifters, many people around us are struggling under the weight of life's challenges—emotional pain, difficult relationships, health issues, or spiritual struggles. Through prayer, we help to lift the load off their shoulders and offer a lifeline when they're too weary to keep going on their own.

To bear each other's burdens in prayer, we must build relationships with honesty and humility. Just as lifters are vulnerable enough to admit they need a spotter to help them, we too must be open with one another about our struggles. Acknowledging our failures and asking for prayer in moments of weakness, allows God to work through our vulnerability and brings us closer to healing and wholeness. This honesty and willingness to share burdens, strengthen our relationships, helping us to become a source of genuine support for one another.

In times like this, prayer becomes a powerful means of support as we ask God to strengthen those around us by providing them with the wisdom and grace they need to endure difficult circumstances. As we lift up others in prayer, we become like the spotter, helping them persevere and encouraging them to hold fast to their faith. God uses our prayers to restore and encourage, to heal and sustain, and to provide spiritual strength when others are weary.

Consider the weight someone around you might be carrying. How can you help ease their burden? Through prayer, you become God's instrument of support, helping to lift the weight they can't carry alone. Together, we can seek prayerful ways to strengthen and build one another up in the Lord, allowing His power to flow through us and lifting each other up as we all press forward in faith.

PRAYER PAUSE

Lord, thank You for the blessing of being able to carry the burdens of others in prayer. Help me to pray fervently and faithfully for those around me. Show me ways to encourage my friends and family as they face difficulties. Amen.

PRAYER POINTS

◆ Praise God for the blessing of close family and friends in your life.

_____

_____

◆ Pray for three people by name who feel alone in their stuggles and trials.

_____

_____

◆ Pray for a personal relationship that needs reconciliation and seek healing.

_____

_____

PRAYER PRINCIPLE

10

Prayer invites God's rescue and peace into our deepest struggles.

— DAY 10 —
Distress Signal

"The righteous cry out, and the Lord hears, and delivers them out of all their troubles. The Lord is near to those who have a broken heart, and saves such as have a contrite spirit."

PSALM 34:17-18

Imagine being lost in a remote wilderness, drifting aimlessly at sea, or stranded on a barren island. Survival becomes a relentless struggle as you face punishing weather, limited resources, and an increasing sense of isolation. It's not long before despair creeps in as hope fades, and eventually, with all other options exhausted, you send out a desperate distress signal. The wait feels eternal, but then—the relief and gratitude you feel when help finally arrives is indescribable. This moment of rescue turns your hopeless situation into one of profound relief and gratitude.

Psalm 34:17-18 reminds us that, in times of desperation, we can call upon the Lord, who hears every cry. Prayer is like a powerful distress signal. When life overwhelms us, when resources run thin, or when we feel abandoned and uncertain of survival, we can call on God, knowing that He listens and responds. This verse encourages us that our cries for help don't go unanswered. Rather,

God swiftly moves to rescue and restore us.

Sometimes our cries for help come from a place of deep heartbreak. Whether from sorrow, pain, or stress, the weight feels unbearable. But here, the psalmist reminds us of God's promised nearness to those who are profoundly broken-hearted. Unlike human rescuers who may be miles away, God is always close as an ever-present help in time of need. He doesn't just watch from a distance; He is near, offering comfort and relief to our souls. His nearness helps lift the heaviness from our hearts, giving us the strength to endure and the hope to move forward.

In those dark times, prayer isn't just about asking for immediate solutions. It's a way of welcoming God's presence into the middle of our despair. His nearness revives weary hearts and restores courage in the face of fear. Just as a distress signal attracts help from a rescuer, prayer draws God into our struggles, bringing peace and guidance where there seemed to be none. We can find solace knowing that God not only hears our cries, but is actively working to bring us relief, even if we cannot yet see the solution.

If you are struggling today, feeling alone or overwhelmed by life's burdens, remember that God is listening to your "distress signal". Your prayers are like a beacon drawing His strength, comfort, and guidance to you. Allow God's constant presence to surround you, filling you with His peace and the strength to carry on. In these moments, we can hold tightly to the truth that God is ready to rescue and restore, no matter how impossible the circumstances may seem.

PRAYER PAUSE

*Lord, thank You for hearing my cries
and for being near in my times of
need. Help me to remember that You
are always present, ready to provide
comfort and strength. Fill my heart
with Your peace and let me trust in
Your faithful rescue. Amen.*

PRAYER POINTS

- Praise God for His compassion and closeness in our chaos and concerns.

_____

_____

- Pray for three people by name who are crushed in spirit and need God's touch.

_____

_____

- Ask God to deliver you from a current problem that is causing you worry and stress.

_____

_____

PRAYER
PRINCIPLE

11

Prayer fuels boldness to live

bravely for Christ.

Shake this Place

"And when they had prayed, the place where they were assembled together was shaken; and they were all filled with the Holy Spirit, and they spoke the Word of God with boldness."

ACTS 4:31

Earthquakes are a powerful reminder of the forces that lie deep within the earth's crust. Without warning, they send shockwaves through the ground, shaking everything within reach. These tremors begin at a central epicenter, but the effects don't stay there. They ripple outward, impacting buildings, landscapes, and lives for miles around. Even people hundreds of miles away can feel the impact of a strong quake from its central epicenter, which reminds us that a single source of power has the ability to shake up and affect everything within its range.

In Acts 4, we find believers praying passionately, asking God to help them spread His Word despite threats and obstacles. They didn't ask for an easy path, but for the courage to face the challenges ahead. In response, God moved powerfully—physically shaking the place they were in and filling them with the Holy Spirit. The prayer that started with a small group of faithful followers didn't just stay within those walls; it rippled out, inspiring boldness and igniting the courage to speak God's Word far beyond that gathering. Their prayers became the epicenter of a movement that would spread out across generations.

Prayer like this doesn't leave things as they were. Just as an earthquake transforms everything in its reach, prayer rooted in God's Spirit changes our hearts, our circumstances, and even our communities. When we come before God with sincere faith, asking for His will to be done, we become the epicenter for His transformative power to begin moving in and around us. As we pray, God may shake up our hearts, stirring up a deeper passion and urgency to reach others and to live in boldness.

But this boldness isn't something we generate on our own. Like those early believers, we are filled with courage through the Holy Spirit, who gives us the strength to act even in the face of fear or resistance. We may find ourselves speaking words of truth and love we didn't know we had, stepping out in faith to serve, or reaching out to share God's grace and goodness with others who need to hear it.

Today, let's pray for God to create an epicenter of change in our hearts. Let's ask Him to shake up our lives with a fresh passion and purpose, allowing us to be filled with the Holy Spirit and empowered to share His Word with boldness. We don't need to create the impact ourselves—our role is simply to pray and invite God's power to move through us, trusting that He will extend the reach of our prayers beyond what we can see.

PRAYER PAUSE

*Lord, shake me with Your Spirit. Fill
me with boldness and faith to reach
others with Your love and truth.
Through prayer, may you ignite a
passion within me to live for Your
purposes. Amen.*

PRAYER POINTS

♦ Praise God for His power that strengthens us to share
the gospel with others.

_____

_____

♦ Pray for three people by name who desire more boldness to witness for Christ.

_____

_____

♦ Pray that God would fill you with His Spirit and shake
up your spiritual life.

_____

_____

PRAYER
PRINCIPLE

—— 12 ——

Prayer enables us to release

bitterness and embrace

forgiveness, reflecting

Christ's love.

— DAY 12 —

Radical Love

"But I say to you, love your enemies, bless those who curse you, do good to those who hate you, and pray for those who spitefully use you and persecute you."

MATTHEW 5:44

In 1956, missionary Jim Elliot and four others set out to share the gospel with the Waorani tribe in Ecuador, a group known for its isolation and acts of violence against outsiders. Tragically, all five missionaries were killed in their efforts, leaving behind grieving families and many questions. Rather than abandoning the mission or harboring bitterness, Jim's widow, Elisabeth, and other families of the missionaries stayed in Ecuador, determined to continue their work with the Waorani. Through their remarkable forgiveness and love, the tribe eventually opened their hearts to the gospel, and many came to faith in Christ. This radical love and commitment to forgiveness inspired countless people around the world and stands as a remarkable testament to the power of Jesus' love.

Jesus' words in Matthew 5:44 call us to an extraordinary level of forgiveness. Loving those who treat us kindly is natural, but responding to mistreatment with forgiveness and prayer, can feel almost impossible. Forgiveness, however, is at the heart of following Jesus, who extended grace even to those who crucified Him. Choosing to love and forgive those who hurt us, allows God to work through us to overcome evil with good, transforming our hearts and situations in ways we could never anticipate.

Prayer plays a central role in this journey of forgiveness. When we come before God with the pain others have caused us, He helps us release our anger and frustration. In prayer, we let go of our desire for revenge and allow God to carry our burdens. Over time, it becomes difficult to remain angry with someone we pray for regularly. God softens our hearts, replacing bitterness with compassion. In this way, prayer frees us from the prison of resentment and positions us to reflect the radical love of Jesus.

When we encounter hurt or mistreatment, we have a choice to make: will we cling to bitterness, or will we trust God to work through the situation? Prayer helps us release control and rely on God's grace to heal our wounds and transform our hearts. Radical love is not about denying the pain others have caused us, but choosing to trust that God can bring something good from even the hardest situations. Elisabeth Elliot and the other missionaries chose to love and forgive, not because it was easy, but because they trusted God's purpose. Through their forgiveness, the Waorani tribe experienced God's love in an unforgettable way.

Consider those in your life who have hurt or mistreated you. Take a moment to bring them before God in prayer, releasing any anger or resentment you feel. Ask God to fill you with His love and empower you to forgive, choosing to represent Jesus even in difficult relationships. This radical love reflects the heart of Jesus and allows us to be conduits of His grace in a hurting world.

PRAYER PAUSE

Lord, thank You for Your endless forgiveness. Help me to release any resentment I hold, filling me with Your love and compassion for others. Teach me to respond with grace, even when it's difficult, so that others may see Your love in me. Amen.

PRAYER POINTS

♦ Praise God for His compassionate love that forgives all of our sin and failures.

_____

_____

♦ Pray for three people by name who have hurt or caused you harm.

_____

_____

♦ Ask God to give you His grace and forgiveness toward others who have wronged you.

_____

_____

PRAYER PRINCIPLE

---- **13** ----

Even small prayers have big potential to unlock God's unlimited plans.

Unlocking God's Plans

"Then the king said to me, 'What do you request?'
So I prayed to the God of heaven."

NEHEMIAH 2:4

Think about the power of a small key. Although tiny, a key has the ability to unlock doors, giving access to valuable treasures or protected spaces. Each key must be precisely machined with the correct ridges and cut to fit a particular lock, granting security and confidence to its owner. Holding the right key to a place, knowing you have both the authority and access, brings a strong sense of security and belonging.

This verse in Nehemiah shows us that prayer can function much like a key. Even the smallest prayers, uttered in the quiet of our hearts, can open doors to God's abundant resources, guidance, and protection. As we look at Nehemiah's story, we see that he was burdened with a desire for his home city, Jerusalem, to be restored. Jerusalem laid in ruins, the city walls destroyed and its people scattered. Nehemiah, though living far away in Persia as a servant to King Artaxerxes, felt the deep call to take action. But before he did anything, he turned to God in prayer and fasting, seeking God's direction.

When the king finally noticed Nehemiah's sorrow and asked

what was troubling him, Nehemiah could have felt pressured to answer immediately. But instead, right in that moment, he paused for a brief but powerful prayer to God. This was a simple prayer, uttered within his heart, but it was a key that opened the door to God's wisdom and provision. With courage and grace from God, Nehemiah made his request to the king, and through God's favor, he was granted permission to return to Jerusalem and rebuild the walls.

There are moments in our lives where we need this kind of small, but essential prayer. Often times, a brief moment of seeking God's guidance in the middle of important conversations, decisions, or even everyday interactions can make all the difference. Like a key that unlocks a door, prayer can open our lives to God's guidance, power, and provision, helping us make decisions that align with His plans.

Nehemiah's brief prayer reminds us that no matter how small our prayer might seem, God hears us and moves through these moments of faith. We may often find ourselves needing direction or wisdom in a situation where we can't stop for a lengthy prayer. But these small, quick prayers have the power to unlock God's wisdom in real-time, giving us insight and guidance. Just as Nehemiah's prayer unlocked the resources of a powerful king to rebuild a city, our small prayers open access to God's unlimited resources.

So, the next time you find yourself facing a closed door, whether it's a decision, a relationship, or an uncertain future, remember that prayer is your key. Even the simplest, shortest prayer has the potential to open the doors of God's plans in your life.

PRAYER PAUSE

Lord, thank You for hearing even my shortest prayers. Help me to trust You in each moment and remind me to turn to You for guidance, knowing that You will open the doors I need to walk through. Amen.

PRAYER POINTS

◆ Praise God that He cares for all the big and small details of your life.

_____

_____

◆ Pray immediately for three people you encounter today who express a spiritual need.

_____

_____

◆ Through prayer, ask God to open doors of opportunity that are a part of His plans.

_____

_____

PRAYER PRINCIPLE

14

Prayer and fasting create a powerful knockout punch giving us victory in spiritual fights through God's strength.

Knockout Punch

"However, this kind does not go out except by prayer and fasting."

MATTHEW 17:21

Heavyweight boxing is not for the faint of heart. The most elite champions are known for their ability to endure grueling matches by building strength, stamina, and strategy. Fighters train for months to prepare for a fight, knowing that victory is not just about brute force, but also about wearing down their opponent with calculated blows. Some of the greatest heavyweight champions employ a signature move—a powerful one-two punch. This consists of a strong body blow to the gut, followed by a swift punch to the head. The result is often a knockout that leaves the opponent on the mat, unable to continue the match.

In Matthew 17:21, Jesus reminds us of the spiritual "one-two punch" available to believers: prayer and fasting. These practices work in tandem, just like a boxer's powerful combination of punches. Prayer aligns us with God's will, giving us the spiritual strength and clarity to understand His purposes. Fasting, on the other hand, brings a level of self-denial that requires full dependence on God, cutting away distractions and heightening our spiritual focus.

In the passage leading up to Matthew 17:21, Jesus' disciples struggled to cast out a demon from a boy. They were confused and frustrated by their failure. When they brought their problem to Jesus, He told them that their lack of faith and inconsistent prayer life was the issue. They had neglected the vital spiritual disciplines necessary for such a victory. Jesus then revealed that some spiritual battles require an intensified strategy—they demand the combined power of prayer and fasting.

No doubt, life can often feel like a heavyweight boxing match. We face relentless spiritual attacks, personal hardships, and trials that can feel like we've been hit in the gut and punched in the face. The weight of it all can leave us feeling like we're on the verge of a personal knockout—ready to throw in the towel. But this verse encourages us that we don't have to fight alone. Through the one-two punch of prayer and fasting, we can tap into God's strength, letting Him fight for us and win the victory.

When we feel overwhelmed by life's blows, it's time to fall back on these powerful practices. Prayer connects us to God's strength and gives us the stamina to keep going. Fasting shows our urgency and full dependency on God in the heat of the battle. Together, they form a spiritual knockout punch that helps us stand firm, even when the fight is fierce. Just like a boxer wearing down their opponent with precision and timing, we are called to fight the good fight of faith with spiritual focus, persistence, and power through prayer and fasting.

PRAYER PAUSE

Lord, thank You for giving me the powerful tools of prayer and fasting to overcome life's battles. Help me to rely on You fully, seeking Your strength in the midst of trials. Teach me to trust in Your timing and power as I engage in prayer and fasting. Amen.

PRAYER POINTS

- Praise God that He steps in to fight our battles when we fervently seek Him.

  _____

  _____

- Pray for three people by name who feel like giving up because of their intense struggles.

  _____

  _____

- Through prayer and fasting, hand over a particularly difficult challenge to God.

  _____

  _____

PRAYER
PRINCIPLE

—————— **15** ——————

Eyes closed shut in prayer gives

us a wide open perspective on

God's power at work.

———————————————

Eyes Wide Open

> "And Elisha prayed, and said, 'Lord, I pray,
> open his eyes that he may see.' Then the Lord
> opened the eyes of the young man, and he saw.
> And behold, the mountain was full of horses
> and chariots of fire all around Elisha."

2 KINGS 6:17

Night vision goggles are a remarkable tool that allows people to see clearly in the dark. These devices work by capturing even the smallest fragments of available light, often undetectable to the human eye, and amplifying it to provide a clear field of vision. With night vision goggles, soldiers and rescuers can move forward with confidence, navigating through the darkness with clarity and purpose.

In a similar way, prayer works as our spiritual night vision, allowing us to perceive God's hand and the spiritual realities beyond what is visible in the physical world. Prayer opens our eyes to a dimension of faith, understanding, and peace we could not otherwise see. The events in 2 Kings 6:17 illustrate this beautifully. When the Syrian army surrounded Israel, panic struck the people. But Elisha, confident in God's protection, prayed for his servant's eyes to be opened to see God's army—a vast, heavenly host with chariots of fire encircling them. In that instant, the servant's eyes were opened, and he saw the unseen defense surrounding them, a reality that calmed every fear and made their enemies appear insignificant in comparison.

Much like night vision goggles enhance hidden light to create a clear view, prayer enhances our spiritual sight, helping us perceive the divine work of God that is often hidden to the human eye. Through prayer, we access a wider view of God's protection, provision, and purpose in our lives. Elisha's prayer teaches us that when we pray with faith, asking God to open our eyes, He responds by letting us see His faithful presence and mighty protection, no matter how overwhelming the situation may appear.

In life, we often encounter situations that make us feel as though we're surrounded by darkness or obstacles. It's easy to feel fearful, anxious, or even hopeless when we look at circumstances from a natural perspective. But through prayer, we can ask God to give us His vision, to reveal the spiritual realities and His purposes that are at work behind the scenes. With this perspective, our fears can be replaced by peace, knowing that God is with us, defending us, and orchestrating events for our good.

As Elisha's prayer was answered, and his servant's fears were calmed by seeing God's armies, so can our fears be calmed when we pray for God's vision. We gain an assurance of His presence and provision that brings peace to even the most challenging situations. Through prayer, our spiritual eyes are opened wide, allowing us to see with clarity and faith that God is greater than any obstacle we face. Let's make it a habit to pray for God's perspective, knowing that through His eyes, we see with confidence, courage, and hope.

PRAYER PAUSE

*Lord, thank You for the clarity You
bring in prayer. Open my eyes to see
Your hand in every situation, and
let my fears be replaced with faith,
knowing You are with me and for me.
Amen.*

99

PRAYER POINTS

- Praise God for how He protects us, even when we don't see or understand.

_____

_____

- Pray for three people by name who are struggling to see God's purpose in their problems.

_____

_____

- Ask God to give you His perspective on the uncertain circumstances around you.

_____

_____

PRAYER
PRINCIPLE

16

*Prayer reaches God, even when
we find ourselves far from Him.*

Anywhere Prayer

"Then Jonah prayed to the Lord his God from the fish's belly."

JONAH 2:1

Noise-canceling headphones are a modern marvel, designed to block out unwanted sounds by adjusting frequencies and creating a calm space even in loud environments. People wear them to tune out the world and stay focused, undistracted by the chaotic atmosphere around them. With these headphones on, someone could be standing in a bustling airport, a busy street, or a crowded café, yet still feel a sense of quiet and focus.

Jonah's experience reminds us of these types of confusing and desperate circumstances of life. Sometimes we may feel that when we're in difficult situations, God is nowhere to be found, that He isn't listening or doesn't care. We might think that God has "canceled" our cries, ignoring us when we need Him most. But Jonah's story shows us that this couldn't be further from the truth. God never cancels out our prayers, no matter where we are or how far we feel from Him.

As a prophet, Jonah was called to deliver a message of repentance to the city of Nineveh, but he chose to disobey and ran away from God's instruction. This led him into a stormy sea and eventually into the belly of a great fish—a place of utter darkness and confinement. Trapped with nowhere to turn, Jonah did the only thing he could: he prayed. And in that moment, despite Jonah's initial rebellion and disobedience, God heard him and responded.

There are times in life when we, too, may feel like Jonah. Perhaps we've ignored God's direction or turned away from His guidance, only to find ourselves in difficult circumstances that feel overwhelming or even isolating. We might feel as though every side is closing in and that no one is listening or willing to help. But Jonah's experience teaches us that even in our deepest distress, we can still cry out to God. Our prayers are not hindered by the barriers, obstacles, or even the spiritual distance we may put between us and God.

In Jonah's darkest moment, his prayer reached the heart of God, echoing through the belly of the fish. The frequency of prayer is tuned directly to God's heart and ears, no matter how far away we are from Him. The obstacles in our lives, no matter how big, do not interfere with God's ability to hear. Just as noise-canceling headphones block out the loudest distractions, prayer allows us to refocus on God and receive His comfort and peace.

Jonah's prayer encourages us to remember that God is never far off, and that prayer connects us to Him in every situation. Even when life feels chaotic and we feel closed in, we can trust that God hears our cries from anywhere. In our times of need, God's presence remains constant, and His willingness to help never fades.

PRAYER PAUSE

Lord, thank You for being near, even when I feel distant or trapped in difficult situations. Help me remember that I can always come to You in prayer and that You hear me no matter where I am or what I've done. Amen.

PRAYER POINTS

♦ Praise God for His grace to accept us when we turn back to Him.

_____

_____

♦ Pray for three people by name who are running away from God.

_____

_____

♦ Pray for God's mercy in an area of your life where you have wandered away from Him.

_____

_____

PRAYER PRINCIPLE

17

*God has placed His people
as prayer ambassadors of
peace over their cities.*

— DAY 17 —

Ambassadors of Peace

*"And seek the peace of the city where I have caused
you to be carried away captive, and pray to the Lord
for it; for in its peace you will have peace."*

JEREMIAH 29:7

An ambassador is a representative who lives in a foreign
land to promote the culture, values, and well-being of
their home country. Though far from home, they work
diligently to uphold the moral and ethical standards of their
homeland, forming diplomatic bridges between nations and
encouraging peaceful relationships. Ambassadors know
that their influence reflects directly on their country, so
they strive to make a positive impact in foreign territories.

As followers of Christ, we are also called to be "ambassadors
of peace," even in places that may feel foreign or challenging.
Jeremiah 29:7 was written to Jewish exiles living in
Babylon—a place and culture very different from their own.
These exiles longed to return to their homeland, and it would
have been easy for them to disengage and withdraw from
their new surroundings. However, God's command through
the prophet Jeremiah was clear: they were to seek the
peace of the city where they were placed and to pray for it.

Their welfare and peace were intertwined with the peace of Babylon, and by engaging as prayerful citizens, they could make a significant impact on the well-being of that city.

This call to be prayerful ambassadors applies to us today, wherever we may find ourselves. God has uniquely positioned each of us within specific families, neighborhoods, workplaces, and cities. In each of these spaces, we have the opportunity to represent the values of our heavenly citizenship—integrity, kindness, peace, and compassion. These values bring healing and reconciliation, especially in places marked by division or discord.

By intentionally praying for the people and places around us, we invite God's grace to transform our environments. Whether it's a challenging workplace dynamic, a strained family relationship, or a neighborhood in need of hope, our prayers can initiate change. Like an ambassador, we bridge the gap between earthly struggles and heavenly peace, representing the love and light of Jesus. Instead of withdrawing from areas that feel "foreign," we can lean in, ask for God's help, and bring His peace into every corner of our influence.

Today, consider the people and places within your sphere of influence that are in need of God's peace. As you pray, remember that God has chosen you to be there as an ambassador of His peace and grace. In your prayers and actions, you reflect the hope of heaven to a world in desperate need of God's love. Let us remember that the peace we pray for others will also result in a greater sense of peace for ourselves, as we align with God's purposes in our communities.

PRAYER PAUSE

Lord, thank You for placing me where I am and entrusting me to represent You in this world. Open my heart to pray for peace in the places around me and to extend Your grace to those who need it most. Help me to reflect Your love and peace in every interaction. Amen.

PRAYER POINTS

- Praise God for the circle of friends and sphere of influence He has placed you in.

- Pray for three people by name who are led astray into worldly pursuits.

- Ask God to help you represent His peace in a broken world.

PRAYER
PRINCIPLE

———— 18 ————

Prayer is not a practice to inform
God but a process to transform us.

A Transformation Process

> *"But when you pray, do not use vain repetitions as the heathen do. For they think that they will be heard for their many words. For your Father knows the things you have need of before you ask Him."*

MATTHEW 6:7-8

Picture a sculptor standing before a large block of marble. At first, the stone looks like an unremarkable mass, rough and unformed. But in the sculptor's mind, there is a vision—a masterpiece hidden within. As the sculptor chisels away each piece, the shape becomes clearer, refined over time with every precise touch. Through this process, the stone isn't informing the sculptor. Rather, the sculptor is transforming the stone, gradually revealing something beautiful and unique.

In a similar way, prayer is meant to transform us. Jesus teaches us in Matthew 6:7-8 that prayer isn't about informing God of our needs—He already knows them. Instead, prayer is about allowing God to shape us, chipping away at the things in our lives that don't align with His purposes. As we come to Him in prayer, we place ourselves in the hands of the Master Sculptor, allowing Him to form us according to His vision.

The sculptor's process is intentional and patient. Each

tap of the chisel brings the sculpture closer to completion, yet the transformation is often slow and subtle. Likewise, as we pray we may not see instant results, but God is steadily working within us, teaching us patience, humility, and faith. The purpose of prayer is not to present God with endless lists or empty words, but to engage with Him genuinely, allowing His presence to shape and refine our hearts.

Just as the marble is changed in the sculptor's hands, we are transformed in God's presence. Prayer invites God to chisel away our doubts, fears, and selfish desires, replacing them with trust, love, and purpose. Sometimes, we might approach prayer with the misconception that excessive eloquence will somehow guarantee an answer, but Jesus calls us to a deeper understanding. He reminds us that God already knows our needs and invites us to pray with sincerity and faith, knowing that each prayer draws us closer to His heart.

When life feels rough or unformed, much like the raw marble, prayer becomes a tool that allows God to work within us. Challenges and unanswered prayers may feel frustrating, but they are often part of the shaping process, molding our character and aligning us with God's will. In those times, prayer is not about "doing" but "becoming"—becoming more patient, more trusting, more like Christ.

So, let us come to God in prayer with open hearts, ready to be transformed. Instead of worrying about saying the right words or repeating our requests, let's trust that our Father already knows what we need. As we yield to His sculpting hand, we can have confidence that He is shaping us into something beautiful, preparing us for His purposes and reflecting His image more clearly.

PRAYER PAUSE

Lord, thank You for being the Master Sculptor in my life. Help me to surrender to Your work. Teach me to pray with sincerity and to seek You not just for answers, but for the growth, peace, and strength that comes from Your presence. Amen.

PRAYER POINTS

◆ Praise God for His wisdom, patience, and artistry in transforming our lives.

_____

_____

◆ Pray for three people by name, that God would work in their lives to bring them closer to His purpose.

_____

_____

◆ Present to God personal areas in need of His refining touch, trusting in His good work.

_____

_____

PRAYER
PRINCIPLE

——— 19 ———

*Persistence in prayer is an
expression of our trust in God's
faithfulness and timing.*

Don't Stop Praying

"Then He spoke a parable to them, that men always ought to pray and not lose heart."

LUKE 18:1

Imagine an athlete who, despite setbacks and exhaustion, presses on toward the finish line. Whether it's a marathon runner pushing through each grueling mile, or a basketball player practicing day after day to perfect their shot, an athlete's journey is marked by persistence. They encounter failures, face moments when giving up feels easier, and struggle against fatigue. But those who ultimately achieve their goals are the ones who choose not to give up, who press on even when the odds seem insurmountable. Their persistence pays off in the end.

In the same way, this verse reminds us of the importance of persistent prayer. Luke 18:1 introduces us to the parable of the persistent widow, a woman who refused to give up despite an indifferent judge's repeated rejection. In telling this story, Jesus encourages us to be like that widow—determined and devoted in our prayers, even when it feels like nothing is changing. Just as an athlete's persistence eventually leads to victory, Jesus assures us that our prayers are not in vain. God hears us, and our persistence moves His heart.

The challenges of life—overwhelming obstacles, pressures, and even crushing defeats—can make it feel as if our prayers are powerless. Sometimes, we wonder if our cries reach God at all. However, Jesus knows our struggles and gave us this parable to teach us that persistent prayer holds immense power. Prayer is not about wearing God down or bending His will to ours, but rather about trusting in His timing, wisdom, and compassionate heart. When we pray without giving up, we are demonstrating faith in God's sovereignty and a reliance on His love for us.

Like an athlete who digs deep within themselves to keep going, we are called to persevere in our prayers, believing that God's purposes will prevail. Persistent prayer is not merely a spiritual discipline; it's an expression of hope and faith in the One who can do all things. Jesus knew that we would sometimes feel discouraged, so He provided this encouragement to remind us that our prayers matter. God listens, He cares, and in His timing, He acts.

As we bring our requests before God, we can remember that each prayer builds our endurance, strengthens our relationship with Him, and brings us closer to His heart. Though answers may not come in the ways we expect, or even in the timing we hope, God remains faithful. We are not alone in our journey and our prayers, no matter how small they seem, have an impact.

So, just as an athlete pushes through pain and fatigue, let us press on in prayer. Let us be persistent, unyielding in our trust in God. He hears every word, He understands every struggle, and in His compassion, He will respond. Keep praying—don't lose heart, for God is near.

PRAYER PAUSE

Lord, thank You for hearing my prayers even when I feel discouraged. Strengthen my faith to keep praying and to trust in Your compassion and timing. Help me to never give up on seeking You in prayer. Amen.

PRAYER POINTS

- Praise God for His faithfulness over time to answer our prayers according to His will.

_____

_____

- Pray for three people by name who are still waiting for a spiritual breakthrough in their life.

_____

_____

- Pray that God would grant you a persistent prayer life to never give up seeking Him.

_____

_____

PRAYER
PRINCIPLE

—— 20 ——

Godly values of devotion,

generosity, and unceasing prayer

cultivate Christ-like character.

— DAY 20 —
Godly Core Values

*"Cornelius was a devout man and one who feared
God with all his household, who gave alms
generously to the people, and prayed to God always."*

ACTS 10:2

Every branch of the military holds its members to a set
of core values—qualities like integrity, honor, courage,
loyalty, devotion, and service. These values unify military
personnel by giving them moral and ethical reference
points that guide their actions and commitments, both
on and off duty. They capture the heart of the personal
and professional conduct expected of those who serve,
shaping their character and influencing their work.

In a similar way, Acts 10:2 introduces us to Cornelius,
a Roman military commander whose life reflected a
different set of core values—those that aligned with
God's heart. Though he held a high-ranking position
within the Roman army, Cornelius displayed qualities
that mark the life of a believer: he was a devout follower
of God, a generous man who cared for those around him,
and a person of persistent prayer. Cornelius wasn't just
dedicated to his duties as a commander; he was deeply
committed to his faith, his family, and his community.

Through Cornelius, God expanded the gospel to reach the Gentiles, beginning with Peter's visit to his home and the preaching of the Jesus. This pivotal moment in history reveals how God used Cornelius's faithful life and prayerful devotion to break down barriers and widen the reach of the gospel. Cornelius's core values of devotion, generosity, and unceasing prayer, opened the door for God's mission to expand beyond the Jews to include all nations and people.

As followers of Jesus, we are called to these same godly core values. No matter our career or vocation, our moral and ethical standards are founded on our identity as members of God's family. Our devotion to God should be evident in every area of life, shaping our actions and priorities as we surrender to His purposes and plans. Generosity should define us as it did Jesus, whose care and compassion were present in every interaction. And a life anchored in unceasing prayer connects us daily to God's promises, enabling us to live with faith and purpose.

These godly core values serve as spiritual reference points to help us focus on God's guidance and goals for our lives. Just as military values unify and guide those in the service, godly values unify and direct us as God's people. In a world that often promotes self-centered goals, these values set us apart and empower us to make a lasting impact for God's kingdom.

Today, commit to developing these godly core values—devotion, generosity, and prayer—as the foundation of your life. Let these values shape your character, conduct, and influence on the world around you, keeping you firmly focused on Christ.

PRAYER PAUSE

*Lord, thank You for the example of
Cornelius. Help me to live with a
devotion that honors You, a generosity
that blesses others, and a prayer life
that draws me close to Your heart.
Shape my character and conduct for
Your glory. Amen.*

PRAYER POINTS

◆ Praise God that His grace and gospel are extended to all people.

_____

_____

◆ Pray for three people by name who are far from God and in need of salvation.

_____

_____

◆ Ask God to develop in you a heart of generosity, devotion, and persistent prayer.

_____

_____

PRAYER
PRINCIPLE

—————— **21** ——————

*God invites us to fervently pray
and faithfully participate in His
redemptive mission in the world.*

———————————————

Recruits for God

"Then He said to His disciples, 'The harvest truly is plentiful, but the laborers are few. Therefore pray the Lord of the harvest to send out laborers into His harvest.'"

MATTHEW 9:37-38

In the year following the tragic events of September 11, 2001, more than a quarter-million Americans with no prior military experience enlisted in the U.S. military. Moved by a call to defend and protect their nation, many left behind established careers, education, and personal plans to become part of a mission bigger than themselves. It was a defining moment, highlighting how, in times of crisis, people can be deeply moved to action. Seeing the need for a united defense, countless individuals committed their lives to public service and a higher purpose.

This image of national enlistment mirrors the heart of Jesus in Matthew 9:37-38. As Jesus traveled through towns and villages, healing and teaching, He saw the crowds and was filled with compassion for their struggles, pains, and lack of spiritual direction. He described the people as sheep without a shepherd, desperately in need of His guidance, mercy, and love. But while there was a great harvest of people longing for God, there were few willing to step up to reach them. His solution? He told His followers to pray for workers to join the mission—to pray that God would raise up more people to bring His hope and love to the world.

Today, this call remains urgent. All around us are people searching for purpose, acceptance, and peace, yet so many are lost without the true hope found only in Christ. The harvest is still plentiful, yet the number of willing workers remains few. Jesus invites us to pray, not only to see the world through His compassionate eyes, but also to be inspired by His heart to take action. He calls us to intercede, asking God to stir up and send out workers. And often, when we begin to pray for God to raise up others, He motivates our hearts to move as well.

Prayer is a powerful step in our mission to bring God's love to those in need. And as we consistently pray for those around us who are far from God, we find ourselves increasingly moved to engage actively in His mission. Just as many were moved to enlist in defense of their country after 9/11, praying for God's mission opens our hearts to participate personally. We become willing to lend our lives to His work, whether through prayer, sharing the gospel, or serving others in love. Our prayers lead us toward action because God often moves us in the direction of our intercessions.

This mission to reach the world for Christ is not limited to pastors or missionaries. God calls each of us, wherever we are, to be part of His harvest. As we pray, may we also be willing to step out, showing His love and compassion in practical ways and pointing people to the hope found in Jesus. Today, let us pray for the salvation of those in our lives and take part in this eternal mission by being willing vessels for His love and grace.

PRAYER PAUSE

Lord, thank You for inviting me to be part of Your mission to reach the world with Your love. Stir my heart with compassion for those who are far from You and give me the courage to step out and serve as Your ambassador. Amen.

PRAYER POINTS

- Praise God that His desire is that none should perish, but all would come to faith in Jesus.

  _____

  _____

- Pray for global missions agencies working to spread the gospel around the world.

  _____

  _____

- Pray that God would use you to help share His love and grace to a lost world.

  _____

  _____

PRAYER PRINCIPLE

22

Prayer has the power to turnaround even the most impossible problems.

—— DAY 22 ——

Turnaround Prayers

*"For I know that this will turn out for my
deliverance through your prayer and the supply
of the Spirit of Jesus Christ."*

PHILIPPIANS 1:19

In 1970, NASA's Apollo 13 mission was rocked by a catastrophic explosion that left the astronauts stranded in space. An oxygen tank had ruptured, crippling their spacecraft and their hope of a safe return to Earth. Thousands of miles away from home, they faced overwhelming odds, with limited power, dwindling resources, and no clear solution. Yet, despite the distance, the Apollo 13 crew had one lifeline: radio communication with mission control back on Earth. Through countless adjustments, specific instructions, and detailed guidance, mission control led them safely through a crisis that seemed impossible to overcome.

Paul's words in Philippians 1:19 echo this idea of a powerful lifeline. Faced with imprisonment and daunting circumstances, he expressed a deep confidence that God would deliver him, thanks to the prayers of others and the steady support of the Holy Spirit. Just as mission control offered the Apollo 13 crew guidance to navigate their crisis, our prayers connect us to the ultimate "Mission Control"

— God Himself. Through prayer, we invite God's wisdom, guidance, and intervention into even the most desperate situations, trusting that He can safely lead us through.

Prayer is not simply a ritual, it's a direct link to God, who has the power to transform even the most impossible circumstances. The Apollo 13 astronauts couldn't have saved themselves. They relied on mission control's knowledge and resources to bring them home. Similarly, when we face problems that feel unchangeable, situations where we see no way out, our prayers invite God to work in powerful ways that we might not have imagined. Through prayer, we acknowledge our limitations and open ourselves to God's unlimited strength and authority.

At times, life may feel like a crisis without an answer, like a problem too big to solve. But prayer is the tool God has given us to call on His help. Just as mission control supplied everything the astronauts needed for their safe return, the Holy Spirit provides us with strength, direction, and peace when we pray. Even if the path ahead is unclear, we can be confident that God's Spirit is present, equipping us to face any challenge.

Today, let's approach prayer with this bold faith. Let's remember that prayer is more than speaking words into the air — it's our connection to the God who guides us through life's most challenging storms, ensuring that He is with us and has the power to turnaround potential danger into pending rescue.

PRAYER PAUSE

*Lord, thank You for being my constant
guide, for listening to my prayers,
and for offering Your help even in the
hardest situations. Help me to trust
You fully, knowing that no matter how
impossible my circumstances seem, You
can lead me through. Amen.*

PRAYER POINTS

◆ Praise God for His limitless power, His constant presence, and His willingness to listen to every prayer.

_____

_____

◆ Pray for three people you know who are facing difficult situations, asking God to guide them with His peace.

_____

_____

◆ Pray about an area in your own life where you feel stuck or overwhelmed, inviting God to bring His solutions.

_____

_____

PRAYER PRINCIPLE

—— 23 ——

God accomplishes extraordinary things through the faithful and fervent prayers of ordinary people.

— DAY 23 —

Mighty Results

"Elijah was a man with a nature like ours, and he prayed earnestly that it would not rain; and it did not rain on the land for three years and six months."

JAMES 5:17

We often hear about the remarkable ministries and accomplishments of well-known Christian leaders like Dwight L. Moody, a prominent evangelist of the 19th century who led countless people to Christ and established churches, Bible schools, and Christian universities. His impact on the kingdom of God is undeniable. Yet behind this visible figure was an ordinary person who made an extraordinary difference: Edward Kimball, a Chicago area Sunday school teacher.

Kimball may not be a household name, but his quiet obedience to God set into motion a spiritual revival that impacted generations. One day, burdened by God's love, Kimball approached Moody, then a young man working in a shoe store stockroom, and shared the gospel with him. That simple act of faithful obedience changed the course of Moody's life and, as a result, the lives of millions. Through Kimball's seemingly small act, God moved powerfully, proving that even the most ordinary people can be used to accomplish extraordinary things. James 5:17 gives us a similar picture of the power of prayer working through "ordinary" people. Elijah was one of the greatest prophets of the Old Testament, known for mighty miracles. But James points out that Elijah was "a man with a nature like ours." He had weaknesses, faced discouragement, and struggled with fear, yet his fervent prayers brought about miracles. This verse reminds us that God does not require us to be flawless heroes; He uses people who are fully surrendered and pray earnestly, allowing Him to work mightily through them.

It's easy to read about Elijah or hear stories of great faith and feel as if we could never be used like that. But the truth is, the power of prayer is not dependent on us—it's rooted in God, who hears and responds. Just as Edward Kimball might not have seemed "significant" in the world's eyes, he trusted God to use his efforts, and God's power flowed through that act of faith.

Today, we can take great encouragement in knowing that God wants to prove His strength through our weaknesses and shortcomings. As we bring our needs, burdens, and desires to Him in prayer, He can accomplish things beyond our imagination. Mighty results don't come from our strength; they come from a great and powerful God who responds to earnest prayers.

Whatever obstacles or challenges you face, bring them to God with the faith that He is listening. Even if you feel small or inadequate, remember that God delights in using those who trust in His ability over their own. In the same way He used Kimball's faithfulness to spark a movement, God can use your prayers to bring about His extraordinary purposes.

PRAYER PAUSE

Heavenly Father, thank You for reminding me that accomplishing great things is not about my strength or abilities, but Your power working through me. Help me to trust that my prayers can make a difference when surrendered to Your purposes. Amen.

PRAYER POINTS

◆ Praise God for His extraordinary power working through ordinary people.

_____

_____

◆ Pray for three people who feel like God could not use them because of their fear or failures.

_____

_____

◆ Pray that God would use your prayers to impact your generation for Christ.

_____

_____

PRAYER
PRINCIPLE

—— **24** ——

*Prayer and praise in the midst
of pain is not our last resort,
but our first response.*

— DAY 24 —

Unshackled Prayer

*"But at midnight Paul and Silas were praying
and singing hymns to God, and the prisoners
were listening to them."*

ACTS 16:25

During World War II, Corrie ten Boom and her sister
Betsie faced harrowing conditions in the Ravensbrück
concentration camp for hiding Jews from the Nazis. Their
barracks were overcrowded, freezing, and infested with
fleas. Despite these grim circumstances, Corrie and Betsie
found a way to give thanks to God—even for the fleas. This
act of gratitude seemed nonsensical at first, but they later
discovered that the fleas kept the guards away, allowing them
to read the Bible and share the gospel with other prisoners.

This story mirrors the account of Paul and Silas in Acts
16:25. After being beaten and imprisoned for proclaiming
the gospel, they were shackled in a dark, filthy jail cell. Their
circumstances were unbearable—physically painful,
emotionally exhausting, and seemingly hopeless. Yet,
instead of succumbing to despair, they chose to pray and
sing hymns to God.

Their response was remarkable. They didn't let their

circumstances define their faith or rob them of their joy. As they worshipped, their voices echoed through the prison, inspiring the other prisoners who were listening. Suddenly, a divine intervention occurred—an earthquake shook the prison, breaking their chains and opening the doors. Yet Paul and Silas didn't flee. Instead, their steadfast faith and love for others led to the jailer and his family's salvation.

This passage reminds us that prayer and praise serve as declarations of our trust in God. When we face trials, we often feel helpless and overwhelmed, but prayer reconnects us to the One who is in control, and praise shifts our focus from our problems to God's power and goodness.

Like these inspiring stories of faith, we too can find reasons to pray and praise in the midst of suffering. When we choose to thank God in difficult seasons, we affirm His sovereignty and allow His peace to fill our hearts. Additionally, our faith-filled response can inspire and impact those around us, pointing them to the hope we have in Christ.

No matter what challenges you face, remember that prayer and praise is not our last resort, but our first response. Praise is not ignoring reality; it's proclaiming the truth that God is greater than your circumstances. When you pray and praise through pain, you invite God's power into your life and open the door for Him to work in ways you may never have imagined.

So, whatever burdens you carry, follow the example of Paul and Silas. Lift your heart in prayer and praise, trusting that God is at work. Your faith may not only bring you freedom but also shine a light for others, leading them to the ultimate source of hope and salvation in Jesus Christ.

PRAYER PAUSE

*Gracious God, thank You for
Your presence in every circumstance.
Teach me to trust You more deeply
and to praise You even when life is
hard. Let my response to challenges
reflect Your goodness and inspire
others to seek You. Amen.*

PRAYER POINTS

- Praise God that He uses pain and uncomfortable cirsumstances to change us.

_____

_____

- Pray for three people by name who are experiencing extreme difficulties and pressures.

_____

_____

- Ask God to give you a heart of praise and prayer in the midst of life's challenges.

_____

_____

PRAYER
PRINCIPLE

—— 25 ——

Prayer is an urgent priority
in a world that is most certainly
passing away.

— DAY 25 —

Urgent Priorities

"But the end of all things is at hand; therefore be serious and watchful in your prayers."

1 PETER 4:7

Imagine being jolted awake by the shrill sound of a smoke detector in the middle of the night. Your heart pounds as you realize that your home is on fire, and every second counts. In moments like this, there's no time to waste on non-essentials. You're not concerned about grabbing your favorite jacket or making sure everything looks neat. Your singular focus is on what matters most: getting yourself and your loved ones to safety as quickly as possible. In the face of such urgency, only the essentials matter.

Peter's words in 1 Peter 4:7 are like a spiritual alarm, calling us to prioritize what truly matters in light of Christ's soon return. Just as the sound of an alarm brings urgency, this verse reminds us of our need to stay focused and engaged in prayer. Prayer isn't simply a habit to fit into our day; it is essential to our relationship with God, especially in a world that often pulls us in many directions and consumes our time with what doesn't last.

Life has a way of filling up with tasks, entertainment, and

obligations that don't carry eternal significance. We can become distracted, even drawn away from God, if we're not careful about our priorities. Peter's words remind us that time is short, and God's mission for us is critical. Prayer is the powerful means by which we align our hearts with God's, preparing us to stand firm, resist temptation, and walk faithfully in our calling. It's through prayer that we experience God's presence, are renewed by His strength, and are given eyes to see His purpose in our lives.

If we find ourselves too busy to pray, it's likely we're simply too busy. And that's when we need to pause and reconsider what holds our attention. Prayer gives us the perspective to see what truly matters and enables us to let go of the things that don't. Rather than letting the world's distractions consume us, we are called to pray with urgency and focus on God's kingdom. As Peter wrote, we are to be "serious and watchful," living with a sense of spiritual readiness. Through prayer, we gain the alertness we need to make the most of the time we've been given.

Prayer allows us to see with God's perspective, and it equips us to share His love and hope with others. As we wait for Christ's return, prayer prepares us to be bold witnesses, ready to share the message of salvation with those around us. This spiritual priority shapes us into people who are awake, aware, and eagerly anticipating the fulfillment of God's promises. Let's answer this spiritual alarm by making prayer our urgent priority.

PRAYER PAUSE

Lord, thank You for reminding me to
stay focused on what truly matters.
Help me prioritize prayer, remain alert,
and be strengthened by Your presence.
Guide me to let go of distractions and
live fully for You, keeping watch until
Christ returns. Amen.

PRAYER POINTS

♦ Praise God that He will one day return and restore all things.

_____

_____

♦ Pray for three people by name who are going through life with spiritual blindness.

_____

_____

♦ Pray about not getting distracted by trivial things and staying focused on God.

_____

_____

PRAYER PRINCIPLE

26

Prayer is God's prescribed remedy
to soothe the sorrows of the soul.

—— DAY 26 ——

Soothing Comfort

"And she was in bitterness of soul, and prayed to the Lord and wept in anguish."

1 SAMUEL 1:10

Life is filled with discomforts that demand remedies. When our bodies ache, we instinctively seek out solutions—pills for pounding headaches and achy muscles, ointments for painful burns, or lotions for cracked, dry skin. Pharmacies are filled with countless options, each promising relief for physical pain and suffering. But what about the deeper aches, the ones that linger in the heart and soul? Where do we turn when the weight of life's sorrows overwhelm us and no shelf holds a remedy for the grief within?

In 1 Samuel 1:10, we find a profound example of this in Hannah, a woman at the breaking point. For years, she struggled with barrenness, a deep wound in her heart that was cruelly exacerbated by the relentless taunting of others. Her soul was consumed with bitterness, and no human intervention or comforting words could ease her pain. Yet, in the midst of her anguish, Hannah chose to turn to the one source of true relief—God. With tears streaming down her face, she poured out her heart in fervent, unfiltered prayer. She knew that only God could fully understand her pain and had the power to do something about it.

Hannah's story reminds us that prayer is God's prescribed remedy for the sorrows of the soul. Just as physical pain drives us to seek relief, life's emotional and spiritual burdens should lead us to seek comfort in God's presence. As Christians, we are not exempt from the trials of this world. We experience broken relationships, betrayal, overwhelming pressures, unfulfilled longings, and personal failures. These struggles can weigh heavily on our spirits, leaving us bitter, anxious, or hopeless. It's in these moments that we face a choice: will we turn to fleeting distractions or worldly advice that temporarily dull the pain, or will we follow Hannah's example and turn to God, who offers lasting comfort?

So, what burden are you carrying today? Is it a lingering grief, a painful loss, or an overwhelming sense of inadequacy? Don't wait any longer to seek God in prayer. Like Hannah, pour out your heart before Him. Be honest, raw, and vulnerable, trusting that He not only hears but deeply cares. Turn away from the false remedies the world offers and place your trust in the One who can truly heal.

God stands ready to soothe your soul and restore your joy. Hannah's story didn't end in sorrow—it ended in the joy of God's intervention and the miraculous birth of her son, Samuel. In the same way, your prayers can lead to the peace, healing, and transformation that only God can provide. Come to Him today and let His presence be the soothing comfort your heart and soul have been longing for.

PRAYER PAUSE

Heavenly Father, thank You for being the God of all comfort, who knows my heartaches and meets me in my deepest needs. Help me to trust You with my sorrows and to seek Your presence above all else. Calm my anxieties, heal my broken heart. Amen.

PRAYER POINTS

◆ Praise God for His gentle compassion and comfort in every bitter and broken moment.

_____

_____

◆ Pray for three people by name who are experiencing deep sorrow and anguish.

_____

_____

◆ In prayer, cast your burdens and worries upon God who provides soothing comfort.

_____

_____

PRAYER
PRINCIPLE

27

*When we seek God
wholeheartedly in prayer,
He listens, responds, and
leads us into His perfect will.*

Seek and Find

> *"Then you will call upon Me and go and pray to Me, and I will listen to you. And you will seek Me and find Me, when you search for Me with all your heart."*

JEREMIAH 29:12-13

The popular kids' game Marco Polo shares its name with the 13th-century Italian explorer. Legend says that Marco Polo had a terrible sense of direction, which is ironic considering his adventures. The game itself is simple—a form of call and response. One player closes their eyes, calls out "Marco," and listens for the responses of "Polo" to guide them toward tagging others. Though their eyes are closed, repeating the calls and responses leads them directly to their goal.

This game provides a helpful picture of prayer. Prayer, like Marco Polo, involves a call and response. We call out to God, trusting that He hears us, and as we listen for His response through His Word, His Spirit, and His guidance, we find clarity and direction in life. Jeremiah 29:12-13 reminds us that prayer is not a game with a distant, hidden God. Instead, it's a deeply relational activity in which God promises to listen and to be found by those who seek Him wholeheartedly.

In the chaos and uncertainty of life, it might feel irrational to think we could find anything of value with our eyes closed. Yet, through prayer, we're led directly to the heart of God. When we call out to Him, He promises to hear us. When we seek Him with all our hearts, He promises that we will find Him.

The context of this verse is significant. Jeremiah delivered these words to a people in exile, far from their homeland and filled with questions about their future. God assured them that though they were in a foreign land, they could still seek and find Him. His plans for them were good, but they would only experience them by turning to Him in prayer and seeking Him earnestly.

Likewise, when we face seasons of disorientation or feel as though we're navigating life blindly, we can trust that God is not hiding from us. He invites us to seek Him, not sporadically or half-heartedly, but with the full engagement of our hearts. Just as the player in Marco Polo finds others by calling out repeatedly, we find God's guidance and presence as we persistently seek Him in prayer.

Prayer is not just about asking for help, but about aligning ourselves with God's will. When we seek Him, He reveals His heart and His path for us by providing periodic course corrections in life. In the process, we grow closer to Him and become more attuned to His voice.

So, even when the way ahead feels unclear, remember this: you're not alone, and God is not hiding. Close your eyes in prayer, call out to Him, and trust that He will guide you. When you seek Him with all your heart, you'll not only find His presence, but also discover His perfect plan for your life.

PRAYER PAUSE

*Lord, thank You for Your promise to
hear me when I call and to guide me
when I seek You. Help me to trust in
Your presence, even when the way
forward seems unclear, and to follow
Your leading with all my heart. Amen.*

PRAYER POINTS

- Praise God for His faithfulness, His attentiveness to prayer, and His unfailing guidance.

_____

_____

- Pray for three people by name who are in the process of seeking God for the truth.

_____

_____

- Pray that God would lead and guide you with His voice through the uncertainties of life.

_____

_____

PRAYER
PRINCIPLE

—— 28 ——

*Abiding in Jesus transforms
our prayers to reflect His heart
and align with His will.*

Abiding in Jesus

"If you abide in Me, and My words abide in you, you will ask what you desire, and it shall be done for you."

JOHN 15:7

The idea of a magical genie in a bottle has fascinated people for centuries. According to the myth, this treasure contains a genie who grants its owner three wishes. The thought of having the power to summon someone who could fulfill any desire stirs our imagination. What would you wish for if you had such a bottle?

Sometimes, we treat prayer as if God were a genie in a bottle, expecting Him to fulfill our every request on demand. However, John 15:7 reminds us that prayer is not about summoning God to satisfy our whims. Instead, it is about abiding in Jesus—remaining connected to Him so that our desires and prayers align with His will.

In this passage, Jesus uses the image of a vine and its branches to explain this truth to His disciples. Just as a branch cannot bear fruit apart from the vine, we cannot bear spiritual fruit unless we remain connected to Jesus. This abiding relationship is the foundation of powerful prayer. When we dwell in His presence and allow His words to take root in our hearts, our prayers are shaped and guided by His purposes.

Unlike a genie who is compelled to fulfill any wish, God is sovereign and wise, knowing what is best for us. Prayer is not about controlling God, it is about aligning ourselves with Him. As we abide in Jesus, His desires become our desires, and our prayers begin to reflect His heart. When this happens, there is no limit to what God can accomplish through our prayers because they flow from a life in harmony with Him.

Consider how a branch connected to a vine receives everything it needs to grow and bear fruit—water, nutrients, and strength—all flow from the vine to the branch. In the same way, when we stay connected to Jesus through prayer, worship, and obedience, His life flows into us. We become empowered to pray boldly, not for selfish gain, but for God's glory and the good of His kingdom.

Let this verse encourage you to see prayer not as a means to get what you want, but as a way to stay in communion with the One who knows and loves you best. The more you abide in Jesus, the more your prayers will become an extension of His will, and the more you will see Him work powerfully in your life.

There is no limit to what God can do when your life is saturated with His presence and His Word. So, remain in Him. Let His words shape your heart and guide your prayers. In doing so, you will experience the joy of bearing fruit that glorifies God and fulfills His perfect plan.

PRAYER PAUSE

Lord Jesus, thank You for inviting me to abide in You. Forgive me for treating prayer as a way to fulfill my desires rather than a way to draw closer to You. Help me to trust Your perfect will, and may my life and prayers reflect a heart that seeks to glorify You. Amen.

PRAYER POINTS

- Praise God for His faithfulness, His attentiveness to prayer, and His unfailing guidance.

_____

_____

- Pray for three people by name who are in the process of seeking truth and meaning in life.

_____

_____

- Pray that God would lead and guide you with His voice through the uncertainties of life.

_____

_____

PRAYER
PRINCIPLE

———— 29 ————

Consistent habits of fellowship,
God's Word, and prayer are
essential for healthy spiritual
growth and maturity.

Healthy Habits

*"And they continued steadfastly in the apostles'
doctrine and fellowship, in the breaking of
bread, and in prayers."*

ACTS 2:42

Our physical health relies on essential practices like eating
nutritious meals, exercising regularly, and getting sufficient
rest. When we neglect these, our health suffers, leaving us
weak and vulnerable to illness. Similarly, our spiritual well-
being thrives when we establish healthy habits that keep us
connected to God and growing in faith. Acts 2:42 highlights
these key habits: devotion to God's Word, fellowship,
and prayer.

When the early church was birthed in the book of Acts, many
people took their first step of faith by trusting in Jesus as
their Lord and Savior. However, spiritual growth doesn't end
with salvation—it requires ongoing commitment. Just as our
bodies need consistent care, our souls need spiritual
nourishment to mature and flourish. This verse serves
as a blueprint for cultivating a thriving relationship with
God and others.

Fellowship is one of these foundational practices.

Gathering with other believers provides encouragement, accountability, and a sense of unity in the body of Christ. It reminds us that we are not alone in our journey of faith. The apostles' teaching, or God's Word, is another essential element. Scripture nourishes our souls with truth, equipping us to live according to God's will and strengthening us against the challenges we face.

Prayer is equally vital. It aligns our hearts with God's purposes, deepens our dependence on Him, and builds our faith. Prayer connects us to God's wisdom and guidance, providing spiritual strength in every season of life. These practices—fellowship, God's Word, and prayer—were not just occasional activities or optional practices for the early church; they were steadfast commitments that shaped their entire lives.

The early church devoted themselves to these healthy habits, and the result was a community marked by joy, generosity, and powerful testimony. Today, these habits are just as important for us. Without them, we risk spiritual stagnation, isolation, and vulnerability to temptation. But when we dedicate ourselves to these rhythms, we experience growth, joy, and a deeper connection to God.

Consider your own life. Are you regularly devoting yourself to fellowship, God's Word, and prayer? Are there areas where you need to reestablish or strengthen these habits? Just as neglecting our physical health has consequences, neglecting our spiritual habits affects our effectiveness for God and our resilience against the pressures of the world. Spiritual health requires consistency and intentionality. Through fellowship, God's Word, and prayer, you will cultivate a vibrant faith that impacts not only your life but also the lives of those around you.

PRAYER PAUSE

*Lord, thank You for the gift of
fellowship, Your Word, and prayer.
Help me to remain steadfast in these
habits, trusting that they will nourish
my soul and draw me closer to You.
Strengthen my commitment to
grow in my faith. Amen.*

PRAYER POINTS

- Praise God for the blessing of fellowship in the body of Christ.

  _____

  _____

- Pray for three people by name in your church who have encouraged you.

  _____

  _____

- Pray about making a commitment to fully participate in fellowship, Bible study and prayer.

  _____

  _____

PRAYER
PRINCIPLE

—————— **30** ——————

Our vertical prayers to God are
impacted by our horizontal
relationships with others.

—————————————————

Access Denied

*"And whenever you stand praying, if you have any-
thing against anyone, forgive him, that your Father
in heaven may also forgive you your trespasses."*

MARK 11:25

We live in a world dominated by passwords. From email
accounts to online banking, passwords verify our identity
and grant access to vital information. But what happens when
a company detects suspicious activity or a possible security
breach? Often, they'll require a password reset, denying
access until the issue is resolved. It can be frustrating, but
it's a necessary step to ensure security and restore trust.

Mark 11:25 highlights a similar concept in our spiritual lives.
Prayer grants us direct access to God, yet our relationships
with others can impact that access. Jesus reminds us here that
unresolved issues, like unforgiveness, can disrupt our prayers.
When we hold grudges or let bitterness fester, it's as though a
password reset is needed for our communication with God.

This verse underscores the importance God places on our
relationships. While we often view prayer as a personal
conversation with God, Jesus makes it clear that our horizontal
relationships—those with others—have a profound influence

on our vertical relationship with Him. When there's friction, God invites us to address it before coming to Him.

Why? Because forgiveness is at the heart of the gospel. God, in His infinite mercy, has forgiven us of a debt we could never repay. To approach Him with unforgiveness in our hearts is to contradict the very grace we've received. Just as God forgave our insurmountable debt through Christ, He calls us to extend that same forgiveness to others. By choosing to forgive, we reflect God's love and align our hearts with His.

It's not easy to forgive. Sometimes, the pain runs deep, and reconciliation feels impossible. But forgiveness doesn't mean excusing wrongdoing or dismissing hurt—it means releasing the burden of bitterness and entrusting the situation to God. When we forgive, we not only free ourselves but also invite God into our relationships to bring healing and restoration.

Think of unresolved conflict as a temporary password lock on your prayers. God isn't denying access to punish you, but to prompt you to address what's broken. When we seek reconciliation, we reset the communication lines—with others and with God.

Take time today to reflect on your relationships. Is there someone you need to forgive? A strained connection that needs healing? God calls us to take intentional steps toward peace, knowing that His grace is sufficient for every hurt and His strength is perfect in our weakness. As you pray, invite God to help you seek out reconciliation with others, offering the same love and grace He has shown you.

PRAYER PAUSE

Heavenly Father, thank You for forgiving me completely and freely through Christ. Help me to reflect Your grace in my relationships. If there's unforgiveness in my heart, reveal it to me and give me the courage to reconcile and forgive. Amen.

PRAYER POINTS

♦ Praise God that He is willing and able to forgive our sins and cleanse us from all unrighteousness.

_____

_____

♦ Pray for three people by name who you need to forgive and seek out reconciliation.

_____

_____

♦ Pray for opportunities to heal broken relationships that have caused you harm.

_____

_____

PRAYER
PRINCIPLE

31

*Prayer is the vigilant watch that
guards our hearts and strengthens
our defenses against temptation.*

— DAY 31 —

A Vigilant Watch

"Watch and pray, lest you enter into temptation. The spirit indeed is willing, but the flesh is weak."

MATTHEW 26:41

Surveillance cameras have become a staple of home security. Easy to set up and connect to Wi-Fi, these cameras monitor our homes 24/7, sending real-time alerts of any suspicious activity. Whether day or night, their unblinking eyes are always watching, recording any motion they detect. They're a valuable tool for safeguarding our homes, ensuring that no potential threat goes unnoticed.

In the same way, Matthew 26:41 reminds us of the vital role prayer plays in our spiritual lives as a "surveillance system" for our souls. Jesus spoke these words to His disciples in the Garden of Gethsemane, where they were struggling to stay awake while He prayed. His warning wasn't just for them but for all of us: watch and pray, because while our spirits may be willing, our flesh is weak.

The world is filled with temptations that appeal to the lust of the flesh, the lust of the eyes, and the pride of life. These distractions and desires can lure us away from God and His purpose for our lives. Without prayer, we leave ourselves vulnerable, like a home without security cameras. Our spiritual defenses weaken, and we become easy prey for the enemy.

Prayer acts as a vigilant watch, keeping us connected to God's strength and alert to the dangers around us. It tunes our hearts to His voice and sharpens our awareness of the spiritual battles we face. When we neglect prayer, it's like turning off our surveillance system—we become unaware of the subtle ways temptation creeps in.

It's important to remember that even with the best intentions, our flesh is still weak. We might think we're strong enough to resist temptation, but without relying on God's power through prayer, our resolve can crumble under pressure. Jesus knew this, which is why He emphasized the need to "watch and pray." In this way, prayer becomes a lifeline that connects us to the strength and wisdom of God.

Setting up a daily "prayer watch" is essential. Like a surveillance camera that operates day and night, prayer keeps us vigilant at all times. It alerts us to spiritual dangers, helps us resist the pull of worldly temptations, and empowers us to stand firm in our faith.

Take time today to assess your prayer life. Are you keeping a constant watch, or have you left areas of your life unguarded? Establish a routine of prayer that invites God's presence and protection into every part of your day. When we rely on His strength rather than our own, we can face temptation with confidence, knowing that He is our shield and defender.

PRAYER PAUSE

*Lord, thank You for being my refuge
and strength in times of temptation.
Help me to stay alert through prayer,
relying on Your power rather than my
own. Guard my heart and mind, and
give me wisdom to recognize and resist
the snares of the enemy. Amen.*

PRAYER POINTS

◆ Praise God for His faithfulness in guarding us, His wisdom to guide us, and His power to sustain us.

_____

_____

◆ Pray for three people by name who are facing spiritual struggles or challenges in their faith.

_____

_____

◆ Pray about areas in your life where you need God's guidance, strength, or protection from temptation.

_____

_____

PRAYER
PRINCIPLE

32

Prayer cultivates the right conditions in our hearts to promote healthy spiritual growth and godly fruit.

— DAY 32 —

Promoting Spiritual Growth

"And this I pray, that your love may abound still more and more in knowledge and all discernment."

PHILIPPIANS 1:9

There's something uniquely satisfying about cultivating a home garden. Watching plants thrive and flourish under your care brings joy and fulfillment. Yet, as any gardener knows, the key to success lies in providing the right conditions for growth. Plants need water to stay hydrated, sunlight for energy, and nutrient-rich soil to anchor their roots and supply essential minerals. If even one of these conditions is neglected, the plant will suffer. Without water, sunlight, or nutrients, a once-vibrant garden can wither and die.

In much the same way, Philippians 1:9 reminds us that prayer cultivates the right conditions in our hearts for spiritual growth. In this verse, Paul prays for the believers in Philippi, expressing his deep care and compassion for their spiritual lives. His prayer is a beautiful example of how we can seek God's help in promoting growth, not only in others but also in ourselves. Paul's desire was for the Philippians to abound in love, deepen their knowledge of God, sharpen their discernment, and bear the fruit of righteousness.

Just as a gardener ensures that each plant has what it needs to thrive, we are called to cultivate the conditions in our lives that encourage spiritual abundance. Prayer plays a vital role in this process. It waters our souls with God's truth, shines the light of His Word into our hearts, and feeds us with the nutrients of His presence and promises. Through prayer, God establishes the fertile ground necessary for love, knowledge, and discernment to grow.

Paul's prayer serves as a model for us to follow. We can intercede for others, asking God to cultivate love and spiritual maturity in their lives. At the same time, this verse reminds us to pray for our own hearts. Without prayer, our spiritual growth, effectiveness, and fruitfulness will weaken and wither. Just as a neglected plant cannot thrive, a prayerless life cannot produce the abundant fruit God desires.

Yet, the promise is clear: an abundance of godly fruit is waiting to burst forth in our lives when we intentionally seek God in prayer. As we create an environment for growth by praying for God's love, knowledge, and discernment to flourish, we will see His Spirit producing righteousness in and through us.

Be encouraged to approach prayer with the same care a gardener brings to their plants. Feed your soul daily with the nutrients of God's presence, His Word, and communion with Him. An abundant harvest of spiritual growth is possible when we make prayer a vital, ongoing part of our lives.

PRAYER PAUSE

Lord, thank You for the example
of Paul's prayer for the Philippians.
Help me to cultivate a life of prayer
that nurtures love, knowledge, and
discernment in my heart. Teach me
to pray for others and to trust You for
abundant fruit in my life. Amen.

PRAYER POINTS

- Praise God for the way He carefully tends to our hearts to produce godly spiritual fruit in our lives.

_____

_____

- Pray for three people by name who are in need of God's love, knowledge, and discernment.

_____

_____

- Ask for three specific needs in your life where you're deficient in the nutrients of God's presence and care.

_____

_____

PRAYER
PRINCIPLE

—— 33 ——

God will move powerfully when
His people are moved prayerfully.

Moved to Action

"*Peter was therefore kept in prison, but constant prayer was offered to God for him by the church.*"

ACTS 12:5

In the early 1900s, George Mueller was known as a man of incredible faith and a champion for orphans. On one occasion, the orphanage staff informed him that there was no food to feed the 300 children under his care. Mueller didn't panic. Instead, he instructed the children to sit at the dining tables as though a meal was already prepared. He then bowed his head and prayed, trusting that God would provide. Moments later, there was a knock at the door. The town baker, who had been awake all night feeling compelled to bake bread for the orphanage, stood there with enough bread to feed everyone. As if that weren't enough, a milkman whose cart had broken down nearby offered all his milk before it spoiled.

This incredible story of God's provision mirrors the truth found in Acts 12:5, where we see the power of prayer in action. At this time, the early church was spreading the gospel of Jesus boldly, yet their faithfulness brought fierce persecution. Believers were beaten, imprisoned, and even executed for their faith. Peter himself was chained and locked in a prison cell under the constant watch of soldiers. The early church could do little to physically free him, but they were moved to pray fervently for his release.

God responded to their prayers in a miraculous way. An angel appeared to Peter, breaking his chains and guiding him out of prison unharmed. When Peter arrived at the very house where believers were praying for him, they were astonished to see him standing at the door! Their prayers had moved the hand of God in a way they could hardly believe.

This passage reminds us of an essential truth: God moves powerfully when His people are moved prayerfully. Just as George Mueller could not meet the needs of his orphans on his own, and just as the early church couldn't free Peter with their own strength, we too often find ourselves facing situations that are far beyond our control. Yet in those moments, God invites us to pray persistently and expectantly.

The same God who provided bread and milk for Mueller's orphans, who sent an angel to free Peter, is still working today. He desires to open doors, remove obstacles, and make a way where there seems to be no way. But He calls us to partner with Him through prayer, aligning our hearts with His will and asking Him to intervene.

When life feels overwhelming, let that be a cue to pray. Prayer is not a passive activity, but an active engagement with the God who holds all power and authority. With God's strength, our prayers can move mountains, change lives, and display His glory to the world. So, call out to God and trust that He is faithful to move on behalf of those who seek Him.

PRAYER PAUSE

Lord, thank You for hearing my prayers
and for being a God who moves
powerfully on behalf of Your people.
Teach me to trust You fully, to pray
persistently, and to believe that You can
do immeasurably more than I could
ask or imagine. Amen.

PRAYER POINTS

- Praise God for His faithfulness to provide, His power to deliver, and His ability to answer prayer.

- Pray for three people by name who need salvation, healing, or deliverance.

- Pray for three personal needs, trusting God to open doors, provide direction, or meet specific challenges.

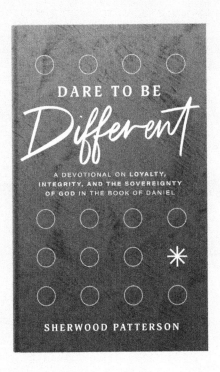

QUEST MINISTRIES

CONNECT WITH US ONLINE

QUESTSD.COM
@OURQUESTSD
INFO@QUESTSD.COM

Made in the USA
Las Vegas, NV
23 December 2024